Understanding the Book of Revelation:

A Commentary on Scripture

Mike Orr

WESTBOW PRESS®
A DIVISION OF THOMAS NELSON
& ZONDERVAN

Copyright © 2019 Mike Orr.

All rights reserved. No part of this book may be used or reproduced by any means, graphic, electronic, or mechanical, including photocopying, recording, taping or by any information storage retrieval system without the written permission of the author except in the case of brief quotations embodied in critical articles and reviews.

All scripture, unless otherwise cited are taken from the Revised Standard Version of the Bible, copyright 1946, 1952, 1971 by the Division of Christian Education of the National Council of the Churches of Christ in the USA. Used by permission.

This book is a work of non-fiction. Unless otherwise noted, the author and the publisher make no explicit guarantees as to the accuracy of the information contained in this book and in some cases, names of people and places have been altered to protect their privacy.

WestBow Press books may be ordered through booksellers or by contacting:

WestBow Press
A Division of Thomas Nelson & Zondervan
1663 Liberty Drive
Bloomington, IN 47403
www.westbowpress.com
1 (866) 928-1240

Because of the dynamic nature of the Internet, any web addresses or links contained in this book may have changed since publication and may no longer be valid. The views expressed in this work are solely those of the author and do not necessarily reflect the views of the publisher, and the publisher hereby disclaims any responsibility for them.

Any people depicted in stock imagery provided by Getty Images are models, and such images are being used for illustrative purposes only. Certain stock imagery © Getty Images.

ISBN: 978-1-9736-6049-1 (sc)
ISBN: 978-1-9736-6048-4 (e)

Print information available on the last page.

WestBow Press rev. date: 05/10/2019

Understanding the Book of Revelation:

A Commentary on Scripture

Mike Orr

Copyright © 2019 Mike Orr.

All rights reserved. No part of this book may be used or reproduced by any means, graphic, electronic, or mechanical, including photocopying, recording, taping or by any information storage retrieval system without the written permission of the author except in the case of brief quotations embodied in critical articles and reviews.

All scripture, unless otherwise cited are taken from the Revised Standard Version of the Bible, copyright 1946, 1952, 1971 by the Division of Christian Education of the National Council of the Churches of Christ in the USA. Used by permission.

This book is a work of non-fiction. Unless otherwise noted, the author and the publisher make no explicit guarantees as to the accuracy of the information contained in this book and in some cases, names of people and places have been altered to protect their privacy.

WestBow Press books may be ordered through booksellers or by contacting:

WestBow Press
A Division of Thomas Nelson & Zondervan
1663 Liberty Drive
Bloomington, IN 47403
www.westbowpress.com
1 (866) 928-1240

Because of the dynamic nature of the Internet, any web addresses or links contained in this book may have changed since publication and may no longer be valid. The views expressed in this work are solely those of the author and do not necessarily reflect the views of the publisher, and the publisher hereby disclaims any responsibility for them.

Any people depicted in stock imagery provided by Getty Images are models, and such images are being used for illustrative purposes only.
Certain stock imagery © Getty Images.

ISBN: 978-1-9736-6049-1 (sc)
ISBN: 978-1-9736-6048-4 (e)

Print information available on the last page.

WestBow Press rev. date: 05/10/2019

Contents

Preface vii

1 - Why We are in the End Times... 1

2 - Revelation 1-5 5

3 - Revelation 6... 9

4 - Revelation 7 & 8 & 9... 13
    The 144,000 Jewish witnesses
    The next seven plagues of the tribulation
    The multitude from every nation

5 - Revelation 10 17
    The Meaning of the Little Scroll

6 - Revelation 11 19
    The Two Witnesses

7 - Revelation 12 21
    The Story behind the Woman and the Dragon

8 - Revelation 13 23
    The First and Second Beast

9 - Revelation 14 25
    The Lamb and the 144,000 from all Human Kind

10 - Revelation 16 27
    The Last Seven Plagues of the
    Tribulation - The Seven Cups of Wrath

11 - Revelation 18 and 19 29
      The Punishment of the Harlot and
      the Mystery of Babylon Unlocked
      The defeat of the antichrist

12 - Revelation 20 33
      The one thousand years of peace and prosperity
      The Imprisonment of Satan
      The Raising of the Martyrs of the Tribulation
      The Last Battle of Satan
      The Resurrection of the Wicked

13 - Revelation 21 and 22 37
      The New Heaven and the New Earth

About the Author 39

Preface

The interpretation of passages in Revelation has been a problem for decades. Many who read it are more confused at the end than they were before they read it. Rome was not built in a day and God does not usually reveal things all at once. The book of Revelation requires reading, backing up, and rereading again and again. Each time it is read a little more is revealed. Meditating and praying are also helpful. God wants us to know the truth, especially now that we are in the last days. Dan 12:9- "Go your way Daniel, for the words are to remain secret until the time of the end." So the Bible deals alot about interpretation. One thing that we must understand in the Bible- there is a physical meaning to each verse and a spiritual meaning. If we do not understand the physical meaning, we cannot understand the spiritual meaning. First physical, then spiritual. 1 Cor. 15:46. "But it is not the spiritual that is first, but the physical, then the spiritual." Understanding can make our face shine. When this happens, you know you have got it right. Ecc. 8:1. "Who is like the wise man? And who knows the interpretation of a thing? Wisdom makes one's face shine, and the hardness of one's countenance is changed."

I have been studying the scriptures for over 40 years and have listened to many speak on the subject, and have read books and blogs on the subject. These are the conclusions that I have made, backed by many references. I do not claim perfect accuracy, but these explanations are the best to my knowledge. Remember to have your Bible handy to follow in the chapters of Revelation, because this is a commentary.

Chapter 1

Why We are in the End Times

Interest in the Book of Revelation and the end times has only started in recent times. In 1970 Hal Lindsey wrote the first book on the subject in a book entitled- "The Late Great Planet Earth." Since then there has been an increasing interest about what is to take place in the future. In the past there have been predictions on when the end will come. In 1843 a man named Joseph Smith predicted that the rapture would take place in that year. And in 1975 another man Mr. Rutherford made the same prediction about that year- causing many of his followers to abandon him. So how do we know that these are the end times? We know through scriptures that are being fulfilled now, that haven't been in the past. If we look at the Book of Matthew in the 24th chapter 32- 35 we see Jesus talking about the fig tree putting forth its branches. This is a sign that summer is near. The fig tree refers to the nation of Israel. In 1948 Israel became a nation. This was to fulfill the prophecy Ez. 37:21 - "I will take the people of Israel from the nations which they have gone, and will gather them from every quarter, and bring them to their own land." The return of Jews to their land signifies the beginning of the end times. In 1967 during the 6 Day War, Israel recaptured the Golan Heights, the West Bank and the Gaza Strip, thus fulfilling the prophecy about the fig tree "putting forth its branches". It also states here that the generation that witnesses these things will not pass away until these things are fulfilled. A generation can last 100 years So the generation born back around 1950 that witnessed these things could be around when He returns. This would imply that His return would be before 2050.

Remember Jesus cursed the fig tree -Mat. 21:19 and the fig tree died and the nation of Israel dissolved and was scattered to all nations -Ez. 39-21-24 but in 1948 they were restored. "And the nations shall know that the house of Israel went into captivity for their iniquity because they dealt treacherously with me. So I hid my face from them and gave them into the hand of their adversaries."

Keeping an eye on the Middle East is key to following the end times as it unfolds.

In Mat. 24:12 Jesus tells us that in the last days wickedness will be multiplied. Dan. 12:4 references this and adds that knowledge will increase- footnotes. Look at all the advances that have come about in the last 70 years: TV, the jet age, the space age, household appliances, advances in medicine, computers, etc. These things did not exist decades ago. This is the fulfilment of prophecy that has unfolded before our eyes.

People are now more evil than ever before. There are more guns than people in the United States, now. 400 people a year are shot dead in Chicago and Baltimore. 30,000 annually are shot. Road rage is everywhere. School shootings are increasing in number and severity. When we watch the news we are watching prophecy unfold before our very eyes. Lawlessness abounds. There are states and cities that do not enforce our federal drug and immigration laws. Cops and ICE are being referred to as Nazis. Jails are referred to as cages. Immigrants storm across our border. Foul language is common- even in congress. In the Book of Timothy in chapter 3 it tells us what people will be like in the last days. "In the last days distressing times will come. For people will become lovers of themselves, lovers of money, boasters, arrogant, abusive, disobedient to parents, ungrateful, unholy, inhumane, un-peaceful, slanderers, shameless, brutes, haters of God, treacherous, reckless, conceited, and lovers of pleasure." Also Ps. 73:1-20. "They have no pain. Their bodies are sound and sleek. They are not in trouble as are others. Therefore, pride is their necklace, and violence covers them like a garment. Their eyes swell out with fatness and their hearts overflow with follies. They scoff and speak with malice, loftily they threaten oppression. They set their mouths against the heavens and their tongue struts through the earth. Therefore, the people turn and praise them and find no fault in them. They say "How can God know?- Is there knowledge in the most high? "Such are the wicked- always at ease. They increase in riches. Then I perceived their end. Truly God has set them in slippery places and has made them fall to ruin. How they are destroyed in a moment- swept away utterly by terrors." Doesn't this sound like today's world?

Also in the last days, there will be many false prophets that will lead many astray. Remember Jim Jones who killed 900 people 40 years ago with cyanide laced cool-aid. Or Rev. Sun Myung Moon who claimed to be Christ. His followers were known as "moonies". David Koresh in Waco, Texas in 1993. Then there was Heaven's Gate. Charles Manson claim to be the son of man. Mat. 24:5 "Beware that no one leads you astray. For many will come in my name saying "I am the Christ" and lead many astray." Also many false gospels are being preached today. Such as the "prosperity gospel". 1 Tim. 4:1 "Now the Spirit expressly says that in the latter times some will renounce the faith by paying attention to deceitful spirits and the teachings of demons." Gal 1:9 "If anyone proclaims to you a gospel contrary to what you have received, let that one be accursed." 2 Tim. 4:3 "For the time is coming when people will not put up with sound doctrine, but having itching ears, they will accumulate for themselves teachers to suit their own desires and will turn away from listening to the truth and wander away to myths."

In addition to the scriptures that I have quoted that describe how people will be in the end times, there are the seven deadly sins-glutton, sloth, lust, pride, envy, anger, and greed. Glutton is easy to see as these sins are on the increase. Today about 2/3 of the population is overweight and 1/3 is obese- 50 lbs. or more overweight. They got this way by stuffing themselves full of junk food. Therefore, obesity, diabetes, cancer, heart disease, and high blood pressure are shortening people's lives. Yes the lifespan is on the decrease. This is true especially of adults. They gorge themselves with pop and candy just like they did as a child only you can't do that as an adult and escape the consequences. When you sin against your body this is what happens. Gal.6:8 "He who sows to the flesh reaps corruption." Lust is also on the increase. Sex is everywhere. They show things on TV and commercials that at one time would be banned through the censors. Anger is on the increase. Road rage school shootings due to population explosion.

In the last 60 years commercial airline flights have made any part of the planet accessible in hours. So more people are traveling to and fro. This also was predicted by the prophet Daniel, Dan 12:5 "But you Daniel keep the words secret and the books sealed until the time of the end. Many shall go to and fro and knowledge will increase. "Going" to and fro" is referring to commercial airline travel. Mat. 24:6-8 talks about birth pains and comparing this to the natural disasters in the last days. What do we know about birth pains. They increase in number and intensity as the birth draws near. Today we see hurricanes, tornados, fires, and earthquakes on the increase, They are bigger now and more intense than ever before. Jesus said that this would be a sign that the end was upon us.

In the last 70 years there have been many strange things going on in the sky such as UFOs, also strange beasts such as Bigfoot, and the Loch Ness monster. Do these mysteries have a common thread? 2 Thes. 2:9-11. "The coming of the lawless one is apparent in the working of Satan, who uses all power, signs and lying wonders and every kind of wicked deception for those who are perishing, because they refused to love the truth and so be saved. For this reason God sends upon them a strong delusion, leading them to believe what is false. Satan is the one who is behind these things. He has lots of time on His hands and likes his fun and games at our expense. People are spending lots of time, even their whole lives chasing rainbows and myths that have no substance.

Hope I have convinced you that we are in the last days- for there has never been a time like today!

Chapter 2

Revelation 1-5

Jesus appears to John and tells him of the things He must show him. First, He describes the seven churches. These are real churches that existed long ago. He lists their high points and their faults that exist in the churches of today. Out of the seven churches, only two were not told to repent. Those two were Smyrna and Philadelphia. Some of the negatives that Jesus referred to were people that claimed to be apostles and were not. I heard of a church once where the pastor told the congregation that he was about to cast out a demon and that anyone who was unsure of their faith should leave immediately unless the spirits should go into them. Well about 95% of the people got up and beat it out the door. Only a small remnant remained in a corner of the church. Well Jesus knows who you are and will spew you out of His mouth, someday. Jesus mentions that some teach false doctrine and that some have lost their first love and need to get recommitted. Now He goes on to mention Laodicea, which is the worst of the seven. These are they that are lukewarm and uncommitted. They are the goats. The difference between sheep and goats is that sheep feed only where the Shepherd directs them- on the Gospel. A goat kind of resembles a sheep. He will feed anywhere and does not discriminate between the world and the Gospel. We are now in the last church period which is Laodicea. These are the ones that Jesus described as wretched, pitiable, poor, blind and naked. They think they see, but are blind. A light can work both ways- it can shine light on a path to direct your steps or it can shine in your eyes and blind you. These people are so blind that they don't even know that this is talking about them. He says that He would rather have them cold (backslidden) or hot (committed) but if they are standing with one foot on the earth and the other in the sea, and then He will get rid of them. Walking on the left side of the road is good and walking on the right side of the road is good, but walking in the middle can get you killed.

There are plenty of false teaching out there today. The one that is particularly common and especially dangerous is the false doctrine of "eternal security". This basically teaches that you can get saved and live in sin and then expect to go to heaven. You are told that you are "sealed" and can't lose your salvation. Heb. 10:26 states "For if we willfully persist in sin after having come to the knowledge of the truth, then there no longer remains a sacrifice for sin, but the fearful prospect of judgement." This is not talking about who sins, falls down and then gets back up and goes running to God. We all do this from time to time. This is describing the person who willfully and persistently sins, and runs from God and delights in in his sin. He has fallen from repentance and goes back to living a life of sin just like he did before he got saved. Reference Is. 59:2 "Your sins have caused a separation between you and your God." This false teaching could send many to hell as it gives a false claim that you don't have to be faithful or accountable to God. Is. 30:10- "Speak to us smooth things, prophesy illusions leave the way and turn aside from the faith- let us hear no more of the Holy One of Israel." Jer. 5:31- "The prophets prophesy falsely the priests at their own accord. My people love to have it so, but what will they do when the end comes?"

After the Laodicean period is over many will come to Christ and preach the Gospel as Jesus instructed in Mat. 28:10. "Go out into the world and make disciples of all men." Acts 2:17-21- "In the last days it will be- God declares- I will pour out my Spirit upon all flesh and your sons and your daughters prophesy, and your young men will see visions and your old men shall dream dreams, even upon my slaves, both men and women, in those days I will pour out my Spirit and they shall prophesy (preach). I will show portents (signs) in the heavens and signs on the earth below (Mat. 24:7), blood, fire, and smoky mist. The sun shall be darkened and the moon will turn to blood (Rev. 6:12 and Mat. 24:29) before the Lord's great and glorious day. Then everyone who calls on my name shall be saved. "This happened on the day of Pentecost but will also happen again in the end times as it describes the darkening of the sun and moon which did not occur at that time. Also a great end time prophet will come who will unite the church and teach a sound doctrine. He will restore the church to a church of commitment and dedication- will be no more Laodicea. He will also reveal who the antichrist is. This prophet is Elijah who came once in the Old Testament and again with John the Baptist, and now once again in the last days. Mal. 4:5 "Low I will send you the prophet Elijah before the great and terrible day of the Lord. He will turn the hearts of children to their parents and the hearts of parents to their children- so I will not come and smite the land with a curse." Mat. 17:11- "Elijah is indeed coming and will restore all things." Rev. 13:18- "This calls for wisdom, let anyone who has wisdom calculate the number of the beast, for it is a human number. Its number is 666." The end time prophet will have this understanding. After the church has been restored, there will be a great falling away. The church will be persecuted and many will betray one another. Mat. 24:9-10- "Then they will hand you over to be tortured and you will be hated by all nations because of my name. Then many will fall away and betray one another and hate one another." This the beginning of the tribulation. The church goes through the first 3 1/2 years and not the full seven that the rest of the world will endure. The tribulation will be shortened for the church by the rapture, which occurs in the middle of the seven years. If this time had not been shortened then no one would be saved. Mat. 24:22- "And if those days had not been shortened, no one would be saved. For the sake of the elect those days will be cut short." The rapture will be discussed a little later.

    Now in Revelation 4 John is taken up and shown heaven, where he sees God on His throne surrounded by 24 elders and 4 living creatures. The 24 elders are said to be clothed in white robes- this signifies that they were redeemed and not angels. They are also said to have crowns. This would signify that they have the crown of life- immortality. They obviously are redeemed humans and quite possibly 12 Old Testament profits and the 12 apostles. Mat. 19:28- "And Jesus said unto them- verily

I say unto you that you which have followed in the regeneration when the Son of Man will sit in the throne of his glory- you shall sit on 12 thrones."

The 4 living creatures are said to give honor to Him who is seated on the throne. They do not have crowns or robes but have eyes on the inside and out- signifying that they see everything that goes on in heaven and on earth. They also have wings that would imply that they are mobile. These are probably angelic creatures because they are not wearing crowns. They signify the four faces of Christ. The first is like a lion- lion is a symbol for a king. Christ is a king. The second is a calf-, which signifies Christ dying on the cross as a sacrifice for sin. The third is human which signifies the humanity of Christ- "Son of Man". The fourth is an eagle. This signifies that Jesus rose from the dead and ascended into heaven. So now you know the mysteries of the 24 elders and the 4 living creatures.

CHAPTER 3
Revelation 6

The next thing John saw was Jesus taking the scroll from the right hand of God. The scroll that Jesus took had seven seals. When Jesus opened the seals they released plagues (judgements) on earth. This begins the tribulation.

The first seal is opened and a white horse who's rider had a bow and came out conquering, and a crown was given to him. This is of course talking about the antichrist, or the counterfeit Christ. Having a white horse means that he will try to appear as Christ, even duplicating some of His miracles- like raising from the dead and breathing life into a statue. He will proclaim himself to be God. 2 Thes. 2:4- "He takes his seat in God's temple, proclaiming himself to be God." He is given a crown- which means he will be given much power and authority, but unlike the real Christ his authority does not come from God. He has a bow but no arrows- no Godly power. He will conquer- will destroy all who oppose him and don't worship him, including the saints. Dan. 8:24- "He destroys the powerful and the people of the holy one."

Now the third seal is opened and out comes the black horse whose rider holds a pair of scales in his hand. This describes a total worldwide economic collapse.

Backing up to the second seal- The second seal reveals a red horse. The red horse is a symbol for blood. He takes peace from the earth- means that there will be a worldwide war.

The next and last is the pale green horse. That's the color your face turns right after you throw up. This is describing a huge world-wide epidemic. It states that a fourth of the earth will die because of this plague.

The fifth seal talks about souls under the alter that cry out for justice. These are the church martyrs- those destroyed before the rapture and are waiting for the Lord. They were beheaded for their testimony of the Gospel and of Jesus. They are told to go back to sleep and wait awhile longer, til the rest of their brethren arrive. They are handed a white robe- meaning they are redeemed. They are said to be "under the alter" which means that they are under the blood of Christ. Alters are what lambs are sacrificed on.

The sixth seal is opened and there is a large earthquake that is felt around the world. This causes the major volcanoes to erupt at the same time sending billions of tons of soot into the atmosphere which traveling across the globe gives the effect of the sky rolling up like a scroll. It also causes the sun to be blotted out and the moon when viewed from the earth, looking through the dust cloud, takes on an eerie, bloody color. This is followed by a huge meteor shower that makes it appear as though the stars are falling to earth. Acts 2:20- "The sun shall be turned to darkness and the moon to blood before the coming of the Lord." Mat. 24:29- "immediately after those days- the sun will be darkened, the moon will not give its light, and the stars will fall from heaven, and the powers of heaven will be shaken." People will be so frightened that they hide themselves under rocks and in caves. This is when the rapture occurs according to Mat. 24:30 "Then the sign of the Son of Man will appear in heaven, and they will see Him coming on the clouds with great glory." So the darking of the sun, etc. that occurred in Mat. 24:29 is the last thing to happen before the rapture. It does not occur before the sixth seal is opened witch means the church will be around until that time. The sixth seal is approximately half way through the entire seven years of tribulation. What else must occur before Christ can come back? One thing is the world-wide preaching of the Gospel. Mat 24:14- "This Gospel of the kingdom will be preached throughout the world, as a testimony to all nations, and then the end will come." One more thing will also happen and that is that the name of the antichrist will be revealed to the church. 2 Thes. 2:3- "Let no one deceive you in any way, for that day will not come unless the rebellion comes first, and the lawless one is revealed."

Now I have described the physical meaning behind the scripture in Rev. 6:12-14. Let me explain the spiritual, for this is really important. The sun being darkened refers to the Holy Spirit being withdrawn from the planet. This signifies the end of the grace period and the beginning of the judgement period. This is when the earth will experience the next three and one half years of extreme peril. The Holy Spirit holds back terrible things from happening to the planet. Such as nuclear war and asteroid collisions. When He is gone, then the earth will be unprotected. 2 Thes. 2:6-7- "And you know now what is restraining him so he may be revealed in his time comes. For the mystery of lawlessness is already at work, but only until the one that restrains him is removed." Zech. 13:7- "Awake o sword against my shepherd, against the man who is my associate- says the Lord of hosts. Strike the shepherd that the sheep may be scattered." This happened after Jesus was crucified when the apostles all ran and hid. It also applies to the last days when the Holy Spirit, who is also God's associate, will be removed and the church will under go persecution. Now going on to "the stars falling from heaven". This is talking about the saints that backslide and fall from grace during the persecution. Mat. 24:12-13- "Because wickedness is multiplied- the love of many will grow cold, but he who endures to the end will be saved." Star is a a symbol for a saint. Dan. 12:3- "Those who are wise shall shine like the brightness of the sky, and those who lead many to righteousness, like the stars for ever and ever." Dan. 8:10- "It (antichrist) threw down to earth some of the hosts and some of the stars and trampled on them."

Chapter 4

Revelation 7 & 8 & 9

The 144,000 Jewish witnesses
The next seven plagues of the tribulation
The multitude from every nation

The rapture has now happened and the church is united in heaven with Jesus. They will remain there for the rest of the tribulation period, which will be 3 1/2 more years. During this time it is believed they will be judged and receive their rewards. 1 Pet. 4;17- "For the time has come for judgement to begin with the household of God..." Now that the church is gone God will set His sights on the 144,000 Jewish witnesses to preach the Gospel to those who remain on earth. He will use the plagues of the tribulation to draw the ones that missed the rapture, to repentance. The witnesses will be protected from the plagues by angels while they spread the Gospel. They have the seal of God on their head- meaning that they are saved.

Next we see the multitude from every nation. These are they that repented after the rapture and have responded to the Gospel and did not receive the mark of the beast. They are martyrs who were beheaded for their testimonies of Jesus. They were handed white robes which means that they were redeemed. The palm branches symbolize that they were victorious. They are too numerous to count, and are from all parts of the world.

In chapter 8 we notice that after the last seal was opened that there was silence in heaven for 1/2 hour. This could be do to the inhabitants of heaven reflecting on what has taken place and what is to happen. A "time out" so to speak.

The next plagues are known as the seven trumpets.

The first trumpet says that 1/3 of the earth; including grasslands and forests will be burnt up. Fires will spread around 1/3 of the globe.

The second trumpet talks about something like a mountain, burning with fire was thrown into the sea- causing a great tidal wave that swamped 1/3 of the ships at sea and 1/3 of the sea became blood, meaning that it could not support life anymore. The mountain thrown into the sea could be talking about the volcanic Island of La Palma in the Canary Islands off the west coast of Africa. It last erupted in 1949. They say when it erupts again it could cause the Island to slide off into the ocean causing a tidal wave so big that when it hit the North American coast, it could travel inland for 20 miles. This could easily explain the disaster described by the second angel.

The next is wormwood- the great star that fell to earth. It appears to be affecting inland fresh waters as opposed to the ocean. People died from drinking the water that was contaminated by the impact. It is described as "blazing like a torch". No other way to describe it. Anyone who saw the movie- Sudden Impact recalls when the asteroid blew over the turnpike it appeared to be a blazing torch. This is obviously an asteroid which impacts a land mass.

When the fourth angel blows his trumpet the heavens are darkened. 1/3 of the sun, moon and stars will be hard to see due to the dust cloud kicked up by the impact of the asteroid.

The fifth trumpet is talking about the release of what seems to be large insects that will attack those who received the mark of the beast. They will torment them for five months, but not kill them. John could not recognize what these insects were because he never saw modern day weaponry- so he described them in terms he was familiar with, such as locusts and scorpions. In reality these are apache type helicopters that have weaponry in their tail section such as lasers or plasma. Area 51 has been working on these for some time, now. These weapons can be modified to burn without killing. It goes on to describe the machines as the size of a horse and on their heads were crowns of gold- this is referring to the helmet that the pilot is wearing. Faces like humans- refers to the pilot. Long hair is to strength- like Samson had. Teeth like lion's teeth- they were very ferocious looking. Scales like armor breast plates- refers to the construction of the craft. The noise of their wings were like chariots. Choppers are very noisy and would produce a similar sound. The devil has authority over them.

After the sixth trumpet sounds, the four demons that when they fell from heaven were imprisoned under the Euphrates river are now released to gather a large army of 200,000,000 to go after and kill a third of mankind. So this army is on "horses". Again John is describing something he has never seen and is describing it in his own terms. The horses are obviously tanks. Lion's heads spewing smoke, fire, and sulfur tanks. This describes a tank firing rounds. This army kills 1/3 of humanity.

Chapter 5
Revelation 10

The Meaning of the Little Scroll

John takes the little scroll from the hand of the angel. A scroll here is a book and books contain knowledge and information. The angel tells John to take and eat it. He said that it would be sweet in his mouth, but bitter in his stomach after he swallowed it. The scroll was the knowledge of what was to pass. The knowledge of what he saw gave him a rush, but it made him sad when he found out that he had to go back and preach the things that he had learned to many people.

Chapter 6

Revelation 11

The Two Witnesses

These witnesses appear during the last half of the seven year tribulation period. They are lamp stands which mean that they hold understanding and wisdom. The city of Jerusalem will be attacked during this time. Dan. 9:26- "And the troops of the prince that is to come (desolating sacrilege) shall destroy the city and sanctuary." The beast makes a covenant with Jerusalem for seven years then in the middle- after 3 1/2 years, he breaks it and sets up the abomination. Dan. 9:27- "He shall make a strong covenant with many for one week (seven years) and for half of the week he will make offering and sacrifice cease and in their place shall be an abomination that desolates."

    The two witnesses will be protected and allowed to preach and if any one interferes, that person will be destroyed with fire. They will be given powers to stop the rains and make the waters turn to blood - polluted. At the end of the 3 1/2 years, when they have finished their mission they will be killed by the beast, but after 3 1/2 days God will raise them up and bring them up to heaven. Then there will be a great earthquake that will kill 7,000 people. The ones that survive will turn to God.

    So who are the two witnesses? They are certainly flesh and blood, because they were killed. They are possibly two Old Testament profits who will be reincarnated to serve God on earth. The two most likely are Moses and Elijah- why? Well both were seen with Jesus after He rose from the dead. Both performed miracles when they were on earth. Moses caused the water to be polluted, and Elijah called down fire on the people at Mt. Carmel. So who are they? We will see what we will see.

Chapter 7

Revelation 12

The Story behind the Woman and the Dragon

Revelation chapter 12 describes a woman who appears in heaven. The woman goes all the way back to Gen. 3:15- "I will put enmity between you and the women- he will strike your head and you will strike his heel." God said this to Satan. The woman is wearing a crown with twelve stars and she is pregnant. Then we see a great red dragon with seven heads and ten horns, seven crowns on the heads Seven is the number of completion. This is Satan. He strikes down 1/3 of the stars from heaven and sends them to earth. These are the fallen angels. Lk. 10:18- "I saw Satan fall like lightening from heaven." The woman gives birth to a son (Jesus) who is crucified and went to heaven. Then the woman flees from Satan into the wilderness where she is protected for 3 1/2 years. This what God meant when He said that he would put strife between the woman and Satan. So who is the woman? It is Israel. Jesus came out of Israel like David did, also. The woman is said to have a crown of twelve stars. These represent the twelve tribes of Israel. Satan entered Judas and Jesus was betrayed and killed and taken out of the way. This satisfies the scripture in Genesis where God said Satan would bruise her head. The head of the woman (Israel). Then by Jesus dying the gates of heaven were opened and now people could be redeemed. This satisfied the scripture in Genesis about the heel of Satan being bruised.

Now Satan suffers another defeat by the archangel Michael and is no longer permitted to go before God and accuse the saints. Now Satan, who must stay on earth is now in pursuit of the woman (Israel). He works through the beast and has seized Jerusalem. This is during the last 3 1/2 years of the tribulation. The woman is said to be given two wings so she could get away from the dragon (beast) and remain in a safe place for 3 1/2 years. This is talking about the evacuation of Jerusalem. They will probably be airlifted by army transport helicopters to a safe place in the desert that was prepared for them. The beast will now send troops out after her (a flood) to sweep her away, but God will intervene and create a large fissure in the earth and it will open up and swallow the troops as they pursue the Jews. It will close upon them and they will be no more- just like Pharaoh's troops were swallowed up by the sea. Now history repeats itself with the beast and the Jews. Rev. 12:16 "But the earth came to the help of the woman, it opened up its mouth and swallowed the river that the dragon had poured from his mouth."

Going back to the beginning of the chapter- it talks about a beast having ten horns and seven heads. This is the same beast mentioned in Revelation chapter 17 that the harlot is riding. The seven heads represent seven leaders that have seven kingdoms. Five have fallen, one is, and one is to come. The one that is to come is the antichrist (beast). The ten horns are ten future kings that have not received a kingdom, yet. These will be the New Roman Empire or European Union. John describes the beast as a leopard. A leopard has spots that make him hard to see- camouflage. This means that the beast will keep his agenda hidden and deceive the world. Its feet were like bear feet This means that he will be unstoppable. His mouth is like a lion. This means that he will say mighty things. Dan. 7:20- "The horn that had eyes and spoke arrogantly." The devil is the one that gives the beast his power. This will be discussed again in Revelation chapter 17.

Chapter 8
Revelation 13

The First and Second Beast

The first beast is the antichrist and is said to come out of the sea. The sea is a figure for the world and politics. He will be the leader of the New Roman Empire, otherwise known as the United States of Europe or the European Union. He will make war with the saints and be given power to do so for 3 1/2 years. There are currently 28 countries in the EU- European Union. In the future there will be ten and the beast will subdue three of them. Horn is a figure for leader. Dan. 7:20- "Concerning the ten horns that were on its head, and concerning the horn which came up to make room for which three of them fell out. This horn had eyes and a mouth that spoke arrogantly, and seemed greater than the others. As I looked this holy made war with the holy ones and was prevailing over them." He will rebuild the temple and take his seat in it, declaring himself to be God- 2 Thes. 2:4. When he does this he will be assassinated- shot in the head and killed. Rev. 13:3- "One of the heads seemed to have received a death blow, but its mortal wound was healed." Then after 3 1/2 days he will rise from the dead and now will be unstoppable. This is the counterfeit Jesus. He will be young like Jesus was and will try and duplicate the things that Jesus did to convince people that he was God. He is the Madhi or twelfth imam which Islam believes is the messiah, but we will know him as the beast. Now when he rises from the dead the people will believe that he is

God and will build a statue of him in his honor. The second beast, the false profit will go over to the statue and breathe life into it, causing it to speak and come to life. Rev. 13:14-15- "It deceives the inhabitants of the earth telling them to make an image for the beast that had been wounded by the sword- yet lived. It was allowed to give breath to the image so that the image could even speak and cause those who would not worship the image to be killed." This being will cause people to receive the mark of the beast Rev. 13:16, which will probably be a computer chip. They can't buy or sell without the chip. The end time prophet will expose the beast and warn the church so they can avoid him. The two witnesses will also warn people. It appears that the beast will battle with the church saints- those before the rapture and after the rapture with the tribulation saints.

The beast will receive his full power of 3 1/2 years after the fir 3 1/2 years of the seven year tribulation.

Now the second beast comes out of the earth. The earth here is the church. This man is a backslider. He gets his power from the first beast and is known as the false prophet. He makes the world worship the beast. He does miracles in the sight of the beast. He makes fire come down from heaven to deceive the people. Rev. 13:13. The fire coming down is probably controlled by a satellite.

Now going back to the first beast. This is the same beast mentioned in Rev. 17. It has 7 heads and 10 horns with 7 diadems. The 7 heads represent 7 leaders that have kingdoms. The diadems are crown that represent authority. 5 have fallen, 1 is, and 1 is to come. The one that is to come is the antichrist. This is the one that receives the mortal head wound. The 10 horns are future kings that have not yet received a kingdom. This will be the European Union. The antichrist is described as a leopard. A leopard has spots that make him hard to see. The antichrist will not make his agenda known, he will be hard to see. His feet like a bear- means he will be unstoppable. A mouth like a lion- means he will speak mighty things. The devil is the one that gives the antichrist his power. These things are referenced in Rev. 17.

Chapter 9

Revelation 14

The Lamb and the 144,000 from all Human Kind

This 144,000 should not be confused with 144,000 Jews mentioned earlier. This is a different group entirely. It says they are in heaven because they are said to sing a song before the throne. The other group was on earth administering the Gospel. This group is said to be made up of the first fruits of all human kind- not just Jews. First fruits means that they were among the first group to get saved- Old Testament profits and early church Christians. These are a special group of saints who have not defiled themselves with women- which means they never were seduced by false doctrine and they follow the lamb wherever He goes- which means that they never strayed or backslid.

The three angels have a message. The first angel warns the earth to repent. This is one reason that God is judging the earth. The other reason is to punish those that wont repent. The next angel is declaring the destruction of Babylon- which will be discussed later. The third angel describes the punishment for those that worship the beast.

Now it goes on to describe Jesus swinging His sickle and reaping the earth's harvest- for the harvest is fully ripe, meaning that all those who are going to get saved got saved. These are the tribulation martyrs. Now they will be raised- this is the first resurrection- not to be confused with the rapture that happened earlier and raise- the church saints. Now another angel declares to Jesus to use His sharp sickle to reap the harvest of the grapes of wrath- those who did not repent. The next seven plagues (cups of wrath) are directed toward the people who received the mark of the beast and would not repent.

Chapter 10

Revelation 16

The Last Seven Plagues of the Tribulation - The Seven Cups of Wrath

The first angel pours out his cup on the earth and those that received the mark of the beast broke out with boils and sores. The second angel pours his cup into the sea and all sea life dies. The third angel pours his cup into the lakes and rivers and all fresh water and they become poison. The fourth angel poured his cup on the sun and the heat from the sun scorched people and they cursed God and did not repent. This happened because the ozone layer, that protects the earth from the strong rays from the sun, had diminished to the point where it could not protect the earth. The fifth angel pours his cup on to the kingdom of the beast and they gnawed their teeth because of their agony and did not repent. The sixth angel pours out his cup on the Euphrates river and the river dries up and lets the 200,000,000 man army- China (kings of the east cross over. Then three demonic spirits like frogs, go leaping forward to gather the leaders of the world to fight the Lord in the valley of Armageddon. The seventh angel pours his cup into the air then violent storms pelt the earth with 100 lbs. hail stones. The stones fell on the people that did not repent and then there was a large earthquake so big that it shook the entire world causing the mountains to crumble to the sea and the Islands in the sea to disappear. Also at this time Babylon is destroyed.

Chapter 11

Revelation 18 and 19

The Punishment of the Harlot and the Mystery of Babylon Unlocked
The defeat of the antichrist

Then John sees a harlot riding a beast with seven heads and ten horns. The seven heads are rulers, five are gone, one is, and one is yet to come. The one that is to come is the antichrist. He will remain a short time- 3 1/2 years. Revelation 13:5- "and it was allowed to exercise authority for forty two months." The ten heads are nations that have not arisen yet. These ten will be the New Roman Empire. The Old Roman Empire fell about 479 BC and was ruled by Charlemagne There currently is a building in Europe named after the former leader. The New Roman Empire is at this time being formed. It is the European Union or "EU". It has 28 countries now and later some of them will pull out leaving 10. This is the ten horns. The antichrist will rule over these- Rev. 17:13- "They are united in yielding their power to the beast." So who is the harlot? Some think it is an apostate church- well I can tell you it is much more than that! Rev. 17:18- "The that woman you saw was the great city that rules over the kings (nations) of the earth. This is a place, not a religion. This country is the chief trader- where all the nations get their riches. It also has become a godless place and persecuted the saints. There is only one place on earth that matches this description and this is the United States. Yes, some day democracy will fall and lawlessness will prevail in this land. Bibles will be banned as hate speech and Christians will be persecuted and killed for being a terrorist cult. Rev. 17 strongly urges those who read these things to repent and come out of her (the harlot) before she is judged.

The beast to the EU to launch an attack (nuclear strike) on the United States. This will last for one hour and will be done with fire. Rev. 17:16- "And the ten horns that you saw, they and the beast will hate the harlot, they will make her desolate and naked; they will devour her flesh and burn her up with fire." Rev. 18:9- "For in one hour your judgement has come." It only takes one hour to destroy a nation with nukes according to what JFK said in 1963 at the signing of the Nuclear Test Ban Treaty. This will be God's final judgement on the United States. We started out as a nation under God and ended up as a harlot- leaving behind God and his principles. It is already starting to get that way now. First amendment religious freedoms are disappearing. Abortion and infanticide- partial birth abortion is increasing. Abortion is human sacrifice to Satan. Our borders are being stampeded by thousands who sneak over here to mooch off of us. Some are criminals and gang members. So far there have been 4,000 murders due to illegals. The man in the white house is doing something about it. This is a national emergency! God is giving us a reprieve, but it wont last for ever. Then lawlessness will take over and we will lose our freedom.

It goes on to explain in Rev. 19 that after the attack Babylon will be completely uninhabitable and completely destroyed. It even goes on to describe how the sailors at sea will pick up the dust from the fall out and toss it up into the air onto their heads. This dust was from the destruction of Babylon. Again it emphasizes the thing that finally caused God to explode on Babylon was the blood of those that were martyred.

Now it goes on to describe the rider on the white horse. This white horse is not to be confused with the white horse in Rev. 6. The rider of this horse is called faithful and true- it is Jesus. It talks about when He returns He will restore law and order to the earth and will rule all nations with a rod of iron. Jerusalem will be the capitol of the world and He will rule over the entire earth. The beast will gather his army to fight Jesus and will be defeated. There will be so many dead bodies that God will gather the birds and beasts to feast on the dead bodies. This is called the "Great supper of God". This happens after the second coming. When He comes back He destroys the armies that ravaged Jerusalem, which are Russia and Iran. Zech. 14:12- "This shall be the plague that the Lord will smite all the tribes that wage war against Jerusalem: Their flesh shall rot while they are still standing on their feet, their eyes shall rot in their sockets, their tongues shall rot in their mouths." Ez. 38:21- "I will summon the sword against Gog (Russia) in all my Mountains says the Lord, the swords of all shall be against their comrads."

Dan 11:40- "At the time of the end the king of the south (Egypt) will attack him (the beast) but the king of the north (Iran) will rush upon him like a whirl wind, chariots and horsemen and many ships." All these will be destroyed by Jesus who will set foot on the mount of olives causing it to split in two. Zec. 14:3-4 - "Then the Lord will go forth and fight against those nations when He fights on a day of battle. On that day his feet will stand on the mount of olives and it will split in two." Jer. 25:33- "Those slain by the Lord on that day will extend from one end of the earth to the other. They shall not be gathered, buried, or lamented, but will become dung on the surface of the ground."

Chapter 12

Revelation 20

The one thousand years of peace and prosperity
The Imprisonment of Satan
The Raising of the Martyrs of the Tribulation
The Last Battle of Satan
The Resurrection of the Wicked

The thousand years of peace and prosperity begin after Jesus returns and destroys His enemies. He he now king of all the world and He takes his seat in the temple in Jerusalem and He along with the saints will rule the whole world. Zech. 14:16-19- "Then all who survive of the nations that have come against Jerusalem shall go up year after year to worhip the King, the Lord of hosts, and to keep the festival of booths. If anyone does not worship then the Lord will not let it rain on their land." He will provide for their needs and heal the sick along with the saints who will be helping. He will destroy those who have ruined the earth- Rev. 11:18- "But your wrath has come and the time for destroying those who destroy the earth." Man has reeked havoc on the earth by polluting the planet and destroying nature. Now this will stop and the earth will go back to a simpler life, like it was in the old testament. Their will be no manufacturing or factories. Things will be made by hand and back yard puddling operations. People will live longer- Is. 65:20 "No more shall there be in it an infant that lives but a few days, or an old person that does not live out a lifetime, for the one that dies at one hundred years will be considered a youth." Also there will be no weapons- He will disarm the world. Is. 2:4- "He shall judge between the nations, and shall arbitrate for many peoples. They shall beat their swords into plowshares and their spears into pruning hooks, nation shall not lift up a sword against nation and neither should they learn war anymore." Another thing that will happen will be Jesus binding Satan and putting him in prison for the duration of the thousand years. At the end of the thousand years he is let out. Rev. 20:2- "He seized the devil and bound him for a thousand years so he could no longer deceive the nations. After that he must be let out a little while."

Next we have the first resurrection- not to be confused with the rapture that took place 3 1/2 years earlier. This resurrection happens after Jesus comes back. In this resurrection the tribulation martyrs are raised. These are the multitude spoken of in Rev. 7. They also will reign with Jesus and the saints during the millennium.

At the end of the millennium Satan is let loose. He immediately sets out to deceive the nations, especially Gog and Magog which is Russia and China. This is a very large army and Satan gathers them to do battle against Jerusalem, but are foiled by God when He sends down fire from heaven which devours them. Rev. 20:9- "They marched up over the breadth of the earth and surrounded the camp of the saints and the beloved city and fire came down from heaven and consumed them."

Now the second ressurection takes place. This is also refered to as final judgement or the second death. This death is said to be final or eternal because there are no more resurrections. The ones that are raised now are the unsaved dead. They are united with their mortal bodies and destroyed by fire. Mat. 28:10- "Why fear man who can destroy the body and not harm the soul- fear God who can destroy both body and soul in hell." The lake of fire appears to be symbolic of termination rather than a real place. Example- death and hades were said to be thrown into the lake of fire and they are not real objects. This means they will come to an end and will not be in the new world that God creats. Rev. 21:4- "Death will be no more; mourning and crying and pain will be no more, for the first things have passed away." So what is the fate of the unsaved. Here are some scriptures that provide the answer- 2Pet. 3:7- "But by the same word the present heavens and earth have been reserved for fire, being kept until the day of judgement and destruction of the godless." 3:10- "Then the heavens will pass away with a loud noise and the elements will melt with fervent heat and the earth and everything that is done on it will be disclosed." Ps. 37:20 KJV- "But the wicked will perish and the enemies of the Lord shall be as the fat of the of the lambs- they shall consume, into smoke shall they cosume away." Mal. 4:1- "See the day is coming, burning like an oven when all the arrogant and evildoers will be stuble. The day that comes shall burn them up says the Lord of hosts."

So now you are probably wondering what could liquefy the earth's crust and destroy everything on the planet? The only possible thing is the sun. The sun could explode into a supernova. The fire from the sun would then engulf the earth until all the wicked and everything on the surface is melted away. This could explain why later in Revelation it is said there will be no more sun. Rev. 21:23- "And the city has no need of the sun or moon to shine on it, for the glory of God is its light." Eventually the sun will burn out and the earth will cool and then having the old earth disclosed God will be able to build a new earth from its foundation. Isn't that the way it usually works? Tear down an old building and build a new one in its place.

So where will Jesus and the saints be when the earth is being burnt? Just like Noah and his relatives were in the ark during the flood, the holy ones will be inside New Jerusalem during the cleansing of the earth.

Chapter 13

Revelation 21 and 22

The New Heaven and the New Earth

The first heaven and earth passed away, now the new earth will be built in its place. Heaven will also be constructed to suit its new arrivals- the saints. The old things have passed away, death is no more. Remember it was said to be "thrown into the lake of fire." The earth will be like it was in the beginning with Adam and Eve- a paradise. Looks like things have gone in full cycle. Also New Jerusalem will come down out of heaven and will be on earth. The saints will be able to dwell in this place. Rev. 21:10- "And in the Spirit He carried me away to a great, high mountain and showed me the holy city of Jerusalem coming down out of heaven from God." The city is described as being a cube of 1500 hundred miles in each direction with a wall and four gates. This is where celebrations and feasts will be held. There will be constant music and colors, no one has ever seen or heard before. Musicians will play their instruments and there will be no more sadness only joy. Also there is no night only day. There will be no time- there is no time in eternity. There will be no past- no one will remember the wicked, for they are destroyed that not even their memory lingers.

Jesus spoke of New Jerusalem to the apostles- Jn 14:2- "In my Father's house are many rooms, if it were not so would I have told you that I go to prepare a place for you. And if I go to prepare a place for you, I will come again and take you to myself, so where I am- there you may be also."

About the Author

I grew up in the 50s and 60s in the Midwest and was raised Catholic. I watched Billy Graham on TV talk about salvation, but did not really make a connection. Then in 1975 my best friend got saved. He introduced me to some of his friends in a metro park. Eventually I got "convicted" and went to their fellowship house and said the sinner's prayer with them and asked Jesus into my life. I moved into their fellowship and started learning a lot about the Bible. I learned more in one hour from them, then I did the previous 24 years of my life, from when I was a Catholic.

Three years later in 1978 I was attending a big meeting out on the east coast, where Stewart, the pastor was giving an end times Bible study. He was showing how to interpret scripture and was translating Mat. 24. It was at that point that I really became interested in the "end times".

Over the years, I have studied Revelation and the books that refer to it. I have also read other people's works on the subject and have listened too many speak on the subject. My book is based on my conclusions.

My book is short, concise, and gets to the point. I am not long winded. I know that after reading the book that many will have questions and criticisms. This is why I am providing contact info so you can correspond with me. I will debate you using scripture and expect that you will do the same- "He who speaks the truth gives honest evidence, but a false witness utters deceit."

My email is- mfoguy£gmail.com

My walk with Jesus has been a rocky road and I have not always been faithful, but He has always been faithful to me- saving my life on more than one occasion. He has appeared to me in a mirror, so I know what He looks like and have no excuse not to believe.

Hope this book is an inspiration to you.

CPSIA information can be obtained
at www.ICGtesting.com
Printed in the USA
BVHW031148200519
548789BV00005B/804/P

9 781973 660491